"In poetic and meditative language, but language which is direct and simple, [Catherine Doherty] invites us to share her pilgrimage. . . .

In a world where noise is almost everywhere, one needs a book like this, not to read in an evening but to have at hand, to use literally as a handbook leading the reader into the sea of silence, helping to reflect on the mysteries of silence, the silence of Christ at all the decisive moments of his life.

This is a book for all, but especially for very busy people. No special learning is required. If one can read the Gospel, one can read *Molchanie*. Those who are weary and a bit battered by life, its pressures and tumult, will find here refreshment and joy."

— James H. Robb, *St. Anthony Messenger*

"...*Molchanie*, the eternal sea of God's silence where the chosen few are called to experience Christ's utter loneliness and where they are first shattered, then gathered into new being. A mystical book born of deep suffering and ecstasy, full of prophetic visions about the Church today, this makes powerful—and disturbing—reading."

— *Library Journal*

"[Catherine Doherty] writes of the silence of God with objectivity: 'An immensity', entrance into which one is free to accept or reject. Her book is also deeply personal, describing a personal journey . . . This is no silence of introspective withdrawal, but of all-embracing Christian evangelism . . . Wherever you are, or whatever work you are doing, 'You can still be imm God.'"

D0877891

Molchanie

Experiencing
The Silence of God

Catherine de Hueck Doherty

MADONNA HOUSE CLASSICS

Cover painting by Patrick Stewart
Molchanik drawing by Patrick Stewart
Design by Rob Huston

Third Edition

Second Printing, July 22, 2009

Second edition, Madonna House Publications, 1991
First edition, The Crossroad Publishing Company, 1982

Printed in Canada

MADONNA HOUSE PUBLICATIONS
COMBERMERE • ONTARIO • CANADA • K0J 1L0

www.madonnahouse.org

Canadian Cataloguing in Publications Data

Doherty, Catherine de Hueck, 1896-1985
Molchanie : the silence of God.

ISBN 978-0-921440-28-4

1. Spiritual Life. 2. Silence. I. Title.

BV4501.2.D65 1991   248.4   C92-090065-8

This book is set in Janson Text, designed by Nicholas Kis of Hungary in about 1690. Its strong design and clear stroke contrast combine to create text that is both elegant and easy to read. Headings are set in Galahad, designed by Alan Blackman as a cross between Optima and the flat-pen writing of Friedrich Neugebauer, the distinguished Austrian calligrapher.

Table of Contents

Preface

In this modern age our minds are like buzzing bees. We cannot hear ourselves think. We are distracted and fragmented. At this time in history we need silence. To be silent we need to be recollected.

Silence is the highest form of communication. But we're not used to it. We don't think of it; in fact we bypass it. We rationalize it away because silence demands discipline. It takes more than just discipline, however, for silence is the fruit of love. Without love, silence is not pleasant—it's aggressive, hostile, negative. But when it comes out of a heart filled with love, then silence really is the highest form of communication.

Perhaps the first step to learn silence may be meditation. We recollect ourselves if we ponder the words of one we love—they might be those of a man or a woman, but in this case they're words of God. As we reflect on their words, we want to meet the person.

There is a mystery about silence. Slowly we begin to set words aside and create within ourselves a quiet heart. We learn to "fold the wings of our intellect," to disengage our thoughts and listen with our heart. Later, much later, when silence born of love has become our companion, we can "unfold the wings" of the intellect again. But at this stage we have to fold them.

Lovers, married people, close friends—all will say that there are moments in their lives when words fall away as if they were old rags—they've become useless. Love cannot deal with them. Love can only deal with silence. It's a silence pregnant with God, filled with love. Wherever there is loving communicative silence, there is God.

It is God who bids us enter into communication. The Father spoke the Word. The Word became incarnate, became a man, our Lord Jesus Christ, who walked among us. He is present among us now; Christ is in our midst. He is this Word that is really the essence of communication.

We go to Mass and receive Holy Communion—we communicate with God. He enters into us and he becomes part of us. This is done so silently. We receive a piece of bread: God. There is silence between two lovers—God and man. The mystery of God meets the mystery of man. This is where real communication begins, when I am in communion with God, with the Most Holy Trinity.

Then I'm in communion with all men. Language is no barrier. Have you ever looked into the eyes of a person who has looked into the eyes of God, and realized that you understood one another? Deep and profound are the wells of silence, and we need it for more than communications. We need it for peace.

There is unpeace in our hearts, and in the world. Why is there violence everywhere? Because we are not silent. We have not lifted our hearts to God. We have not communicated with him. We have not taken inner counsel with one another. That is to say, that counsel that comes from the union of love.

How many of us are silent enough to listen to the other? When one is listening and another talking, people begin to understand each other; and then this can be reversed and the one listening can begin to talk. We don't listen because we have no inner silence of mind or soul.

It is not easy to be silent, but it is necessary if we are to begin our journey inward to meet the God who dwells within us. Jesus Christ said, "My Father and I and the Holy Spirit will come and dwell within you." Once we meet Them our silent communication with Them will transform us into icons or images of Christ. Do our hearts not hunger to bring forth God through our silent communication with Him?

As St. Augustine says, "My heart is restless until it rests in Thee." Silence is always restful. But silence also becomes a cradle. Silence is the cradle of the Incarnation of God. There was a great and awesome silence when God was born.

I make a cradle out of my heart for any one of you to rest in like a child. As Christ said, "Unless you become like little children you shall not enter the kingdom of heaven." That's why my favorite prayer is: "Lord, give me the heart of a child and the awesome courage to live it out as an adult."

Silence is also an inn. There was a Good Samaritan who picked up the man besieged by robbers. Who of us is not besieged by robbers today? Who of us does not need an inn where all is rest and peace and silence? This is what silence does; it becomes the highest communication, the quickest way to peace, the cradle for a child, an inn for the weary and tired.

Silence produces all this if you and I fall in love with God. For it is out of that love, that fantastic union that only God could devise for us, that silence can become all those things.

What does the world need most of all? It needs to touch God. Through silence I realize that I can touch Jesus Christ everywhere. Silence is the key to many secrets of God. Why don't we ask Him to give it to us?

"For when peaceful stillness compassed everything and the night in its swift course was half spent, Your all-powerful word from heaven's royal throne bounded, a fierce warrior, into the doomed land. . ." (Wisd. 18:14–15)

The Word, Jesus Christ, comes when peaceful silence encompasses everything, when the night is half-spent. I may refuse to enter into the night of inner quiet, of non-resistance to the divine. If I do refuse, my life is doomed to remain parched and lifeless.

What is this silence that constantly prepares for the coming of the Lord? Silence can be understood in many ways. Silence can be experienced as the absence of noise. Silence may also mean the absence of words that are needless. The absence of useless talk, the softening of a voice that is shrill and strident. The cultivation of silence belongs to the gentle style of life. A style permeated with what we are and what we do.

One dimension of a gentle lifestyle is that of speaking and not speaking. Speech is a wonderful thing, but what source does it spring from? Insecurity makes one talk, talk, talk, so as to impress the next person.

Psychiatrists say that gossip belongs to the insecure, for it makes us feel important for a few minutes. Love can make us capable of silence.

Today people are hungry for friendship, for understanding, for someone to talk to, someone who really listens. But who of us ordinary mortals can really listen with the ear of the heart wide open, taking in every word that the other says? The weight of listening is heavy.

That is why we need to pray for a "spiritual bulldozer" to make straight the ways of the Lord in our hearts, so that He might come unencumbered and do the listening in our hearts. So that He might understand, console, help, those who come to us!

He will do it through us if we reduce our interior noise to a gentle silence that listens to Him. He will do it if we stop the swirling dust of our mutterings, our non-listening to our brother. He will come especially when we allow this spiritual bulldozer to really make straight the paths of our hearts for Him to walk on unencumbered, so that he can listen through us, talk through us, understand through us.

Sometimes we speak anxious and tense words interiorly to ourselves, words that drive us toward moralistic self-perfection. These powerful, unspoken words can be more harmful than spoken ones, for they halt the one Word that wants to fill my life.

To reduce our noise, to become silent, is to enter His silence, and His silence speaks. There is no renowned spiritual master, from the East or the West, who did not praise the silence that leaves room for presence to *the Presence*: God himself.

When you have cried out to God for the gift of the prayer of silence, then you plunge like a deep sea diver into the tremendous sea of God's silence. You totter on the edge because it's kind of frightening, but prayer will get you over the edge. Dive deep and allow the silence of God to touch your silence. Two silences will meet, and then all things are seen in their true light.

Ultimately prayer is union of a person with God. It's a bridge. Then comes a time when even prayer does not exist, in the sense that we usually understand it. There is a total silence of a person before God. Then suddenly, at the moment of this strange silence, God invades the heart. And when God has invaded the heart, who needs to pray? For God is within, totally, completely.

Silence
Is a dark night
Where first
The soul
Meets its death to self.

> Where noise
> Cannot abide
> Not noise of word
> But thoughts.

> > Silence is a school
> > Of Love and death
> > That leads to
> > Light.

Silence
Is a dark night
Where
Soul and mind
Abide
To wait
For light
That is God's Speech.

Silence
Is a school of
Love and death
Where soul
Meets life.

Silence
Is the key
To the immense
Furnace of Love—
The heart of
God.

Silence is
Speech
Of passionate love
Spent
In the arms of God.

Silence
Is—
One-ness
With the Lord!

Perils of the Sea of Silence

Molchanie in Russian means "silence," and this book is about the silence of God and about our entry into the silence of his heart. The experience is something like being hit with lightning.

Some people may actually begin their life journey within the silence of God, for he so attracts their hearts that they cannot resist. They allow him to enter and make his abode in their hearts. But God reveals his silence to very few persons during the early years of their life. Most people must go through stages in their walk with God.

I've written three books describing a life journey: first *Poustinia*, (Russian word for "desert," a place set apart for encountering God), then *Sobornost*, (Russian for a particular kind of "unity," in and with God), and finally, *Strannik* (Russian for pilgrimage). One goes first into the poustinia of the heart to allow God to cleanse oneself thoroughly, that is, to cleanse one's soul of all that is not God, so that, purified, one becomes united with God, in sobornost. Then the Lord will tap one's shoulder and say, "Now is the time to go on a pilgrimage, into the sea of silence."

On this pilgrimage one must walk through a desert where nights are cold and days unbearably hot, where there are all sorts of strange insects and animals. Imagery, you say! Yes, but who can describe what happens to people who spend a long, long time in a desert?

As they pilgrimage the Lord leads them slowly towards the sea of silence. From a silvery beach he bids them plunge into his immense silence. You enter this sea and it covers you, yet you don't drown for the Lord does not want anyone to drown. With profound faith you allow yourself to sink gently into his sea of silence.

This is an unusual sea, one in which a person, as he continues to descend, loses all fears, even fear of death and fear of God. In this infinite sea, into which a person plunges out of love, he discovers Love: God. The desert and the silvery beach are portals to the sea of silence through which those who are called must enter.

They will truly experience God's embrace of love, but also his 'embrace' of trial. For this is not yet the parousia, the second coming of Christ! When one enters the immensity of silence, one meets loneliness and rejection.

Have you ever known loneliness? It has a thousand faces and is never the same, and it becomes your companion in the sea of silence. It will never leave you. Although it might disappear for a moment or two, it will return, because the loneliness at your side is that of Christ.

Can you endure the utter loneliness of Christ? Consider his loneliness at the time of the Annunciation, when the Holy Spirit overshadowed Mary, and the Child began to grow in her womb. Consider the loneliness of the Child, the Youth, in St. Joseph's workshop. Then his departure from home and his lonely walks throughout

Palestine. Now you are beginning to understand his utter loneliness.

Finally, his silence before Pilate and his loneliness on the cross. When you stand beneath the cross, you will see loneliness itself. It will have a face, and it will look into your eyes. If you have reached the foot of the cross in your silence, then you have begun to understand the loneliness of Christ. One cannot understand the sea of silence unless one also understands the loneliness of Christ.

So prepare yourself. For you will begin to understand that this loneliness is only another way that the Triune God uses to purify your soul. You see, the Trinity dwells within you—Father, Son, and Holy Spirit. From within your heart and soul they will breathe forth the infinite power which is their life. But for this to happen, you must be ready to accept loneliness.

When we reach the silver sands and plunge into the great sea of God's silence, we begin to understand that he alone is God. He is lover, friend, and the totality of gentleness, peace, and rest. He calls us and we cannot resist his call. We have to be alone with him. It is a necessity, a hunger. Christ walks with loneliness and rejection, and so must we.

Yes, rejection was also the constant companion of Christ. It walked with him from the moment of his conception until the moment of his resurrection.

While he was on earth his words were often rejected. A few of his disciples received them, but his words were rejected by the Jewish elders and High Priest. Christ's words were rejected by many of the people he loved.

When people saw him hang from the cross, most lost all faith and hope in him. Oh, a few women stayed with him, as did St. John. There were some Romans who *had* to be there. That was the sum total of the entourage of the Great King. Yes, he walked in the shadow of rejection all his life.

We do not take rejection easily; we fight against it. In fact, we are ready to leave the silvery beach and the sea of silence, because somewhere deep down in our hearts arises a reaction to rejection: anger. It is demonic and a fruit of the Evil One.

Anger is the opposite of peace, and peace is what the person who has entered the sea of silence lives by. In the arena of the soul a new struggle begins between peace and anger. God has permitted it and he alone knows when it will end. Anger is like some gem–laden ornament that we grab, which suddenly turns into a thousand snakes. That is what anger is, snakes that well up from the bottom of our souls to bite, to hurt, to kill.

Christ accepted rejection and forgave those who rejected him. We don't. The snakelike creatures that form deep down in our souls prevent us from forgiving. In the sea of God's silence, which is the baptismal water of Jesus Christ, we must forgive everyone so as to overcome the snakes of anger and hatred. This forgiveness will be a crucifixion. But Christ prayed for those who hurt him; so did the saints, and so must we.

If we love God, we shall be able to look upon rejection as a great blessing. Christ will share with us the excruciating pain of it, and through that will teach us how to love our enemies. All this we will learn in the sea of silence.

Within those infinite depths into which you plunge out of love, your learning will continue. You will absorb lessons of pure, total love, a love that knows no bounds. You will understand how to love your enemies. Yes, and the anger that so often welled up within you will slowly vanish in those deep waters of the Lord's sea. You will know anger no more.

Yet loneliness and rejection will continue to be your companions: you will be lonely and rejected as Christ was, with the terrible accompanying pain. You may even be rejected by your friends, but certainly by your enemies.

When I first came to North America I didn't have many friends, but I had many enemies. People rejected me because to them I was just another "Polack." I leave it to your imagination how a foreign–born person lives with rejection. Only by the grace of God—but, oh what a grace!

Praise the Lord with me, for rejection is a great gift of his love! Can you imagine who Jesus Christ becomes to those who are rejected like he was? We share in his rejection. Dance! Let the music sound! The Son of God was totally rejected. Where is our place, the place of those who profess to love him? On the other side of his cross!

Do you know what happens when you accept rejection? A very simple thing. Our Lord takes you off the other side of the cross, tenderly kisses you, puts you in the arms of his mother, and bids her to be the Good Samaritan who pours oil over your wounds. She takes you home and consoles you. Now you know, as few people know, two things: the kiss of Christ, and the nursing love of his own mother. What more could we possibly desire?

In the poustinia, then, God cleanses the soul from everything that is extraneous to himself. This eventually leads to union with him (sobornost), but this union is not yet complete. It will be completed when the soul that loves him so passionately is willing to enter the silence of God.

Don't think that those who enter the silence of God are "silent." Nothing could be farther from the truth. Molchanie is a thunder! You will be able to hear it everywhere. Your nights and days will be filled with it. You will be able to hear nothing but the thunder of God's silence.

Those whom God calls into his silence will enter a vortex which will shatter them into little pieces. Looking here and there you will see fragments of a human being. You will behold your own fragmentation and wonder why you do not die. I do not know why. God knows. But in his silence he will gather together your fragments. And when you emerge from the sea of silence you will become like thunder, thunder that passes beyond the galaxies as if it were a bird sent forth to preach the gospel to the whole universe.

Many confuse silence with *solitude*. Solitude is something quite different from silence. Solitude is being alone with God, waiting for God. But silence is an immense sea into which you enter and never leave.

So don't mistake silence for solitude. Silence does not depend on your being alone. Whether you are in a streetcar, in a church, teaching a class, or working on a computer, you can still be immersed in the silence of God. If you are immersed in this silence, the little things you do—cooking meals, cleaning house, working in office or wherever—all will be a thunder that spans the divide between sun and moon.

You may not realize it yet, but preaching the gospel emanates from the poustinia. The poustinia creates a unity with God, and then causes a confrontation with the world. You may be martyred but, like a phoenix, you will arise again and again. Like Christ, you will arise from a crucifixion.

Oh, people are not going to crucify you with nails and hammers. No, they will crucify you with words, with mockery: "Look, he believes in God, he believes that Christ is divine!" This will be worse than being crucified. But you will endure it, for the great silence of God will become a thunder all around you.

God has entered your heart through his silence. Having put together your fragmented self, he now tells you to go on pilgrimage to preach his gospel through a silence that is more powerful than any words you have ever spoken. Yes, of such elements is silence made.

Silence is more powerful than any words, except one: *the* Word, our Lord Jesus Christ. It is by entering into the Word that the gift of utter silence, and therefore of complete speech, is given to some.

But silence also has a dimension that doesn't belong to the Word. Silence does not necessarily lead to peace and closeness to God. No! Silence can also be a temptation, coming from the Tempter himself. Satan is allowed to tempt us by false silence so that we might discover what true silence is. I will give you a few examples.

One can barely hear the water that some slave is pouring over Pilate's hands. That was done in utter silence. The Jews and Romans listened with bated breath to that deathly sound of water, that was no sound at all.

Many stood there, allowing this false silence to enter their hearts. Some, I am sure, wrapped their cloaks around themselves and walked away. This silence of injustice was unbearable.

There is the silence of a cruel death. I remember that when my husband and I were starving in Finland (I have described this in other books), silence was all around us. But it wasn't the silence of God. It was the silence of the Tempter. My husband and I went to sleep; there was nothing else to do. We were allowed to have good, fresh water, but water alone does not sustain you for long.

So we went to sleep. Don't ever try to escape into the silence of sleep, unless you are really sick and can sleep in a sort of emotional vacuum. Otherwise, don't. Take it from me that when you are starving and you sleep in order to escape silence, silence finds you—but not the silence of God. It is the silence of the Tempter, who laughs in your face and presents you with many tempting dishes.

We went to sleep. I don't know what my husband dreamt about, but I dreamt of succulent meats, lovely salads, the beautiful cold melons so beloved by the Russians. When we woke up and tried to orient ourselves, it seemed as if we heard in the distance a diabolical laughter. For he had finished with us, or so he thought; he had left us in the utter silence of his living hell, and he was content.

But God had other plans! We were saved from that hellish silence.

Should you wish to experience this kind of silence you can go into the alleyways of the world and see old women rummaging through garbage cans, and children collecting what you have thrown away. The poor go about this task in a despairing silence, crying silently to God. People have closed their hearts to these poor. Walk through the garbage alleys of the world and you will know the silence of Satan. In that silence one of two thoughts will emerge; either, "Will I share more with the poor?" or, "To hell with the poor!" What effect will this silence have on *you?*

Silence can lead us to God, and that is why the Evil One constantly tries to interfere with it. Take, for instance, the harmful silence of indifference, which I described in this poem.

Silence

Silence is a wall
Made of black,
And coiled stone
Like a snake

Immovable
Inscrutable
Silence has stood
Cool
Aloof
A wall without a roof!

Men have hurled
Bodies and souls
Against
Its blackness
Hardness
And have died trying!

> Bodies and
> Souls
> Broken and dead
> Lie at the foot
> Of the black
> And cold stone
> That silence is. . .
> Am I one of them?

There is a silence which doesn't say a single word, negative or positive. It's a silence whose very nature is to deny what it believes, or to deny everything. How many people throughout the ages have entered this silence! They didn't actually bear "false witness." They simply entered the silence of denial. They stood in front of those who questioned them, without saying anything. They just stood there, mute witnesses to their tragic denial.

Perhaps in their ears echoed the words of Christ: "He who denies me before men, I will deny before my Father." Did these silent ones understand what they were doing? As one looks at the course of history, it becomes quite clear that there were many such silent ones.

But what type of silence is it that does not refute, does not deny, that turns man into a stone? Peter denied God three times, but then he went out and wept when the cock crowed the third time. Did these people hear the call of the cock? (Luke 22:54–62)

In Russia I once came upon a man whom the Communists were questioning about his belief in God. He became like a stone, in no way indicating whether he did or did not believe in God. Finally someone asked him, "Will you deny your God if you believe in him?" There was no answer. Perhaps I didn't hear the answer.

As I walked down the street (this happened on a street where members of the Red Army, who were half drunk, were, in a manner of speaking, teasing the man more than interrogating him) I realized that in our own century, a lot of us only professed to believe. Oh, we went to church. But our deeds were opposed to our beliefs.

This sham belief is the reason for all the cults today. Youth walks the earth, silent searchers for the Absolute. They do not find the Absolute (God) because the majority of believers have entered, not God's silence, but the silence of the Tempter. He can change a human being into a stone, so that the grace of the Lord cannot penetrate into him.

When I was small we lived for awhile in Egypt and my parents took me to see the beautiful stone statues of the kings. My father was six–foot–two and a half, but even he looked short in front of those huge statues of the Rameses.

Last night, in the dark warmth of Arizona, I couldn't sleep. It seemed to me that my father had been holding my hand and pointing out, not these huge statues, but a tragic forest of stonelike people who by their silence denied their beliefs.

I dozed and then woke up with a great fear, almost a panic. I went to the little altar we had in the house and prayed that these stone people might open up to receive the love of Christ. Again I fell asleep. But throughout the night I knew that men were turning into a forest of stone. I knew that man was free to say yes or no to this silence. When once more I awoke I heard the voice of

Christ, saying, "He who denies me before men, I will deny him before my Father."

Come then, let us run hand in hand into the deep sea of silence and into the sea of rejection and loneliness, and laugh at Satan. He thinks this sea will drown us. He is wrong. Christ has conquered!

Plunging into the Sea

Just before plunging into this infinite sea of mystery and love, at the brink of entering its depths, one's soul is poised and reflective. It's as if God were asking it, "What is your choice?" and standing there waiting for an answer. God waits! Isn't it awesome that man can make God wait? But he does.

Memories of his long pilgrimage pass before the pilgrim's eyes. They are closed, for he listens. Somewhere out of the past, out of the infinite silence which is the Lord's speech, he remembers the voice that called, "Arise, my beloved, my beautiful one, and come!" (Song 2:10) He remembers that at one time—he has almost forgotten when or where—he arose and followed that voice throughout a long, long pilgrimage until he finally arrived at these silver sands where he is now, deciding how to answer God's question.

He stands face to face with God and remembers how he started out in some poustinia and there saw the face of God, although never as fully as he desired. Then God called him to a pilgrimage that few people accept to go on. He went through untold hardships and untold delights before finally arriving at these silver sands where the waves lap the shore.

Here God asks the question: "Will you accept the vocation of silence?" It is not the vocation of living alone. No. It is the vocation of entering the sea of infinity to preach the gospel in deep silence, and by preaching the gospel silently, drawing an innumerable host of people towards God.

The silver sands are warm; the sun shines on them in a very special way. I and a few others stand there, looking at this beautiful, shimmering, sun–reflecting sea, which during the night reflects the moon and stars. It especially reflects the infinity of God.

The time has come to plunge, yes, to take the plunge into this deep and immense sea that is the infinity of God. There is no other sea like it; it is the sea of his heart. Those who hunger and thirst to be alone with him are the ones invited into it.

Listen! Hear the waves lapping on the shore. Each wave says, "Come, come, come." And we have to go. Not because we are impelled by anything human. No, we are impelled by love, a love that knows no bounds. Even if our love is still 'bound,' in a little while it will be like Christ's—boundless. Like Christ, we will open our arms to embrace the whole world: all peoples and races, and even our enemies.

There is no hesitation now in our hearts. We lift our eyes and it's as if God smiles down upon us. The next thing we know we are entering the warm waters of the sea, which are the waters of baptism made holy by the presence of Christ. Only now they have become this immense sea, which seems to cover everything, because God is infinite. And with the ears of our souls we hear the voice of our God: "He who has given up everything for Me will receive a great reward."

How the sea beckons! We have already gone in up to our knees. Now up to our waists. Now up to our necks. And then, like one who dives into a wave, we willingly plunge into the very depths, because he who loves us is in the depths. In time we will be one with him, and the Christ in us will embrace the whole world.

Be at peace, be at peace. It is a time of waiting. Be very quiet, very quiet. For now we must hear the words of God coming from the depths. Listen very carefully! For here, out of the depths, he will begin to teach us how to become totally identified with himself.

The silver sands are gone. So is the mountain that was in the background. There is nothing now except water. Is it water, or is it the infinity of God's mercy and God's power? The step has been taken. Everything has been left behind. Nothing, nothing remains.

Those of us who have jumped into the infinite waters of God come out somewhere onto a shore that has no sand or mountains or sun. It is rough country. There are sharp stones, boulders, and knolls that seem part of a larger mountain whose summit cannot be seen. Are we supposed to walk over these sharp stones? Is it for this that we left the silver sands? Is it for this that we plunged heedlessly into the warm sea of God's mercy? The sharp stones barely form the outline of a path leading upwards. But the voice whispers, as if from afar: "Come. I am waiting for you. Come."

Walking barefoot over sharp stones we pilgrims of the Absolute, who are searching for God with our whole being, follow this barely visible path of silence. We did not know it would be so harsh. We did not know it would be so lonely. No matter. We have to go. The silence of God draws us on like a lover draws his beloved.

It doesn't matter if we leave bloody footprints along the way. Nothing matters except our entry into God's silence. We have met his silence before, as well as the silence of Satan and of indifference. We have understood a little bit—not much—of the loneliness of Christ and of his rejection.

As we slowly walk this stony path, which cuts the soles of our feet, we hear from somewhere the voice of the Tempter: "Turn back!" But we can't; we must go on to meet God. Then we hear another voice, clearer and more powerful than the first: "If anyone thirsts, let him come to me; let him drink who believes in me." (John 7:37–38).

We realize that it is we who are hungry and thirsty, and we are astonished that we have come so far in following Christ. We fall on our knees and cry out, "Lord, have mercy on me."

Then before our very eyes Christ appears. In his one hand is a cup of wine and in the other, a piece of Jewish flat bread. He hands me, and those with me, the chalice—a wooden cup. He tears the bread into pieces so that each of us has enough. We eat and drink, and fall asleep.

When we awake there is no bread and wine, but we are refreshed, and we now have the strength to move upward over the terrible stones, over briers and thorns which try to hold us back. With quiet, slow, firm pace we move forward. He who has received the bread and wine, food for the day, has been consoled by Christ.

As we move quietly and simply up the stony path, a new mystery is revealed to us. The consolation we have received we must pass on to others. This consolation is the Good News that God loves us. The faith, hope, and love of our hearts pass over into the hearts of others, and they are consoled.

Now we know why we followed Christ into such great silence: to experience how one grows strong in Christ by being fed by him. We understand also that our silence now covers the whole world, because it is not ours, but his.

Here I would like to share a poem I once wrote.

Silence and Atonement

My heart
And I
Have
Learned
Silence
Today.

It took us
Very long
To understand
That silence
Is part
Of the domain
Of Lady Pain.

That there
Are courts
And stairs
And turrets
And chambers
Without end

In the domain
Of Lady Pain.

And that
My heart
And I
As we grow
Will
Surely and slowly know
(Because we
Are yet fairly
Small...
And not quite
Learned as
Yet in all
The ways
Of pain
And love)
Spend some
Time
In every court
And walk
Each steep
Step
Of every stair
And enter

Turrets
Chambers
One by one
And stay in
Each...
Until each

One
Has taught
My heart
And I
Its lesson
Of pain,
Its chant
Of love.

And then
Some day
We do
Not know when
My heart
And I...
Will
Find

The
Last
Strange
Ladder
That
Will
Bring us
To final
Ecstasy
And death
That starts
A life
Of endless
And eternal
Delight.

But that
Is not yet
For we
Must
Learn
To suffer
And to wait...
To hide
From all
The
Facts
That

Now
We live
In two
Domains
That of
Earth
And that of
Lady Pain.

We are
So slow
My heart
And I...
To learn
Anything
At all...
And yet
Today
We learned
The art

Of silence
When in pain.
We learned
That the skins
Of a white doe
Bind tight

And that
They increase
The pain
A hundredfold
Yet silence
Must be kept.
We tried
So hard
Today
When we
Were crucified.

And now we know
That pain
Borne
For Love's
Sake
Is like
A flame
That brings
Us in
The very Heart
Of pain
And then
Dips
Us into

The infinity
Of peace
That
Sends us
Back Again
Into
The heart
Of pain...

Yes, silence
Taught
Us much today...
We learned
That love
Must have
Its way
And never count
The cost
We paid the cost
In silence
And in joy
While in the very
Heart of pain.

Somewhere I was sitting on the grass, picking daisies. I was pulling off the petals, saying, "He loves me, he
loves me not." Suddenly, two people were at my side.
They seemed to be transparent. You could see through
them, or so it seemed.

They were not picking daisies; they were talking to
one another as well as to me. I had not been thinking of
anything "spiritual" at that moment. I was playing this
game with God. I really knew that he loved me; still, the

daisies were so sweet. I enjoy playing games like this with God.

One person was saying, "I am God's Solitude." The other was saying, "I am God's Silence." Solitude said that she was the friend of God, much more important than the Silence of God. And so they went on, arguing between themselves.

I said, "Don't you know that the silence of God is quite different from solitude? You seem to have come from the place where God abides, yet you have not understood this. The silence of God is his love given to someone who walked to the silver sands, to the edge of the sea of infinity. He was drawn with his whole being to enter this sea, and he did enter it. The silence of God is nothing else than the complete following of Christ.

"This silence of God is pain beyond measure. Those who enter are plunged into God's knowledge, God's healing, and God's power. Have you forgotten that when he said, 'Love one another as I have loved you,' he made us heirs, children of the Father? At the same time, to those few who entered his silence, he gave his own knowledge, and the power to heal and to bring people to him. And have you forgotten that all these powers rest on the very slender thread of faith, on which silence also rests?

"Solitude usually walks with silence, but silence does not need solitude. Silence possesses solitude in itself. He who enters the depths of God's heart leaves solitude at its door, because the silence of God envelops him. Solitude is a way of silence. It can lead to the silver sands, but it does not necessarily plunge one into the infinite sea of tremendous silence, pain, joy, crucifixion, and resurrection.

"Solitude prepares a person for silence, prepares him to approach the silver sands and jump into the waters of the sea. Then solitude leaves the silver sands and walks again the rocky pavements of city and country, calling, whispering, proclaiming God to anyone who will listen.

"Slowly, solitude gathers a small group that she will lead to the silver sands. Solitude will, however, lead others into the busy marketplace, where they will serve the poor, the sick, and the lonely, just as the Lord served us. Solitude will console. Solitude will enter families and bring peace where there is strife. Solitude has much work to do, and one of these works is to bring a small group of people to the silver sands at the edge of the immense sea."

When I finished saying all this to the two who were sitting at my side, they vanished.

Entrance into the silence of God is not a matter of thinking. It is an action. You stand on silver sands and then move into that sea of infinity. You must plunge deeply into it. There is no bottom; its depths will continue to reveal themselves during the rest of your life.

This sea can also turn into a mountain at God's command. So, sometimes, in the great silence of God you are not swimming but climbing, climbing slowly and painstakingly toward its invisible summit. This is covered with a sweet and beautiful fog like you sometimes see in early morning in the fall. That's how the summit appears, but you reach it only when you die.

In the immense silence of God, be it the sea of infinity or the mountain, you must go on, because the incredible has been revealed to you—God's overwhelming love, for you and for all. You cannot resist his love.

You continue onward, whether in depths of the sea or on heights of the mountain. Love is a magnet that will not release you.

The only difficulty is that the deeper you go into the sea, or the higher you go up the mountain, the clearer do you see before you the desires, hopes, and dreams of mankind. They are laid out like a map, with all its plains and contours and mountain ranges.

From the very beginning of the human race, men and women disobeyed God. However you wish to understand the story of Adam and Eve, one thing is certain: somewhere deep down in the heart of man is disobedience to God.

Somewhere deep down in this same heart is the urge to kill. Let that truth sink into our hearts. Cain killed his brother, and this is what people have been doing since time immemorial—killing one another. Today you not only see people killing each other, but you see more; men are torturing one another.

Over all this pain, touching the sky and rooted deeply in the silence of God, is a cross made out of wood. The Son of God hung on this wood, on this cross full of splinters. Flies crawled all over his wounds, and the crown of thorns allowed no rest for his head.

On this cross, God bleeds. Is that the result of an imagination running wild? I don't know. But I see that in each person who dies by the hand of his brother, in each person who is tortured by another, Christ bleeds. Christ is in eternal agony. There is no respite for him. War follows war. In the depths of his silence God opens the eyes of my heart.

I turn my face away for a moment to blot out the sight, but still I see him who sat and talked to the

Samaritan woman. I cry, because his pain has been my pain for so long. He answers me from the throne: "Catherine, until the end, until we meet, you will experience my pain. But then you will sit forever at my feet and experience my joy."

Hope is a gift of God. It appears when everything else is lost and when hopelessness seems to reign. The deep silence of God hovers over you, even when the landscape that surrounds his silence is bleak.

One stands in the midst of sheer cliffs that cannot be climbed through human effort. From below, all one can do is look up at these immense cliffs, which seem to touch the sky. Of course, there is a distance between the cliffs and the sky, but because one is so deep down into the silence of God, cliffs and sky seem to touch. The cliffs of hopelessness are steep and slippery, and thy seem to grow taller.

But having stood by the silver sands and jumped into the abyss of the infinite sea, one is no longer merely human, and therefore hopeless. Hope must spring from somewhere, and it springs from God.

This is the moment of trust. Can God provide you with a ladder to climb to the top of these cliffs? Prayer seems impossible, and the Tempter assails you on all sides. Faith alone has hold of you, as if by a small hook and slender wire. You have to pick up the hook and wire which are lying at your feet, and attach them to yourself. You hook them on to your ragged clothes. Quicker than a streak of lightning, you feel a tremendously powerful tug on this slender wire. As you experience his power, Christ laughs.

Did you ever hear Christ laugh? He used to dance and clap his hands like all Jewish children. I don't know if he danced as an adult, but he must have danced when he was a youth. In the immense silence you can hear the clapping of his hands, and the laughter of God.

Hope surges in your heart as you are carried up, up, back into the big wide world of sun and moon, of beautiful trees and lovely flowers. It is because this gives Christ such great delight that he laughs.

That's how it is. But, alas, people do not believe in God's power. One after another, they jump off bridges and take sleeping pills. I myself experienced the temptation to despair. In my book, *Fragments of My Life*, I talk about these temptations. Water can look inviting and peaceful from the top of the Brooklyn Bridge. There were many, many times when I stood at the feet of sheer cliffs and couldn't see the hook and the wire to which I could have attached myself. Yet it was always there— barely visible perhaps, but always there.

However, in the great silence of God, even when you cannot pray with your lips because they are cold and you cannot pronounce the words, the words are pronounced by your heart. And the prayer of your heart always is, "Have mercy on me, Lord, for I am perishing—perishing because I don't seem to believe in you. My faith is weak; strengthen it!"

Once you have experienced the powerful tug of God lifting you out of seeming hopelessness, nothing in this world will ever again cause you to despair. Even the experience of martyrdom, I don't think, would bring you to that. Martyrs receive special graces from God.

And so, on this thin hook and wire you surface into the fresh air. You lie down peacefully in a garden. The Wind, which is part of God's silence, passes by and whispers to you, "That was one of the tests. God tested you and did not find you wanting."

Mysteries of Silence

The road became steeper and the stones sharper. Clouds hung low over the stony path so that one could barely see it. A storm was brewing. I moved slowly, as one heavily burdened, though the only thing I carried was a shepherd's crook to help me walk.

I came across a group of men screaming, yelling, and gesticulating. Two or three of them were dragging a half–naked woman to where Christ was standing. I was deeply engrossed in silence and really didn't want anything to do with this scene. My silence seemed to be a warm protection against the coming storm.

The woman was crying. I tried to make a detour, but there always seemed to be somebody in my way. So I stopped. I heard her accused of adultery, a crime punishable by stoning according to Jewish law. They were yelling at Christ too.

In an unusual gesture, he bent down and began writing something on the sand; he was absolutely silent. So was I—utterly silent. Suddenly he stopped writing and broke the silence by saying, "If any one of you is without sin, let him cast the first stone." Then he continued to write.

The quality of silence changed. Flashes of lightning seemed to explode around me. Kneeling on the sharp stones, I knew, with a knowledge no one could ever take from me, the *mercy of God*. One by one the men left her, until the woman was left standing there alone. Christ broke the silence once again: "Woman, is there no one to condemn you?" "No one, Lord," she replied. "Neither will I condemn you," he said. "Go, and don't sin any more."

She left, but I remained. Christ ceased writing on the sand. He sat down on a large stone and looked at me. I looked at him. Breaking my silence, I said, "Lord, I have just witnessed the immense mercy of God. Will I die for having seen it?" For I was absolutely sure that no one could behold this outpouring of mercy that flashed like lightning, and remain alive.

The Lord shook his head and smiled and said, "No, Catherine. That is not what you are here for. You are here to become a silent witness to this mercy. Now that you have had it burnt into your soul, now that you know what mercy is, *go and be merciful.*"

The sharp stones disappeared. The little path was not there any more. In its place was a beautiful garden, with olive trees in bloom. Coming toward it marched a group of men brandishing arms, and although the garden was someone's property, no one seemed to oppose their arrival. They passed over a small knoll, opened the gate of the garden and entered.

All came to a halt, and out of their midst sauntered a man who was not armed. He walked straight towards Christ, who stood a short distance ahead of those who were with him in the garden. Then this man, putting his arms across Christ's shoulders with a sort of gentle hug, kissed him on both cheeks. It seemed at that moment that the earth stood still; there was not the slightest breath of wind anywhere. The silence of nature penetrated my heart like the silence of a funeral.

The armed crowd seemed to sense this, too. They kept looking to the right and to the left, as if trying to locate this silence that enveloped everything.

I leaned against a tree, for I felt too weak to stand up without support. I was beholding the betrayal of God by man. It was not the betrayal of a nation by a nation. It was not the betrayal of one family member by another. Oh, no! It was the betrayal of God by man.

To my amazement, nothing happened. I was not close enough to see if Jesus returned the kiss. I simply know that Judas said, "This is the man."

After that I entered into a great silence, and only bits of conversation drifted past me. Almost no one spoke. It was like being in the midst of a void. There was only one booming thought, which seemed to cover everything with death: God had been betrayed by man. And by a man who knew who he was! Betrayed by a man who had been with him for almost three years of his public life. Betrayed by a man who was his close companion. Yes, this was the only thought which penetrated the void of my silence.

The crowd passed me by as if I were not there. I walked on. On the occasions when the High Priest or Herod or Pilate were speaking to Christ, I seemed to be in a corner someplace, listening. But I couldn't hear anything. Nothing penetrated the void of silence in which I lived. The void itself was inflicting pain on me—pounding into my head like a crown of thorns the words, "Man betrayed God; man betrayed God!"

Somehow I arrived at Golgotha, stood before the cross, and beheld God crucified. His head was slumped forward, the crown of thorns askew on his head, causing intense pain. I did not dare lift my eyes often. Finally the strange void of silence fell away, loosening the grip of its terrible embrace.

I looked at Christ and it seemed as if I had grown taller, so that when he lifted his head and looked at me, our eyes were on the same level. I was going to say something, but his voice broke the silence first. It was strong, even though coming from a crucified man.

He said, "Catherine, yesterday you witnessed the mercy of God. You saw Our mercy and you thought that was the whole of it. No, child, the mercy of God is infinite. I shall pray to my Father." He cried out, "Father, forgive them, for they do not know what they are doing." Then he looked at me and for a split second I thought I saw a smile on his face.

Then he went on: "Now, Catherine, you have seen the immensity, the infinity, of God's mercy. Go and be merciful to everyone, but above all, *be merciful to your enemies.*"

Silence returned then, enveloping me like a beggar's cloak. I looked at myself and saw that I was poorly dressed, much as Russian pilgrims are. My dress was so beggarly as to be almost disgraceful, and my long skirt was catching hold of the prickly plants as I passed. I wore a black "pilgrim's shawl," for it was cold. (Silence is sometimes cold.) The shawl was clasped below my chin with a large thorn.

Slowly I travelled a path that led to a large city. The path became a wide road and then melted into innumerable streets. No one seemed to pay any attention to this old woman in a black shawl, ragged dress, and old slippers. Several streets came together at a kind of plaza, with park benches scattered around it. I was becoming tired and sat down on a bench.

Soon I became lost in the vast silence of God, and could only dimly hear the noise of passing traffic. The silence of God is all–absorbing, and I was plunged into it.

Suddenly a beggar appeared out of nowhere. His pants were ragged, frayed at the ends. He had long hair, which shone a little, even though there was no sun. He wore a woolen tunic and had something on his shoulder. Perhaps it was a water gourd, for it was rather flat.

I looked at him and he at me. Then every time someone passed by this little plaza, he arose and put out his hand, asking for alms. It reminded me of the days of the Great Depression, when people were begging five cents for a cup of coffee.

He never said anything, but only extended his hand. Each time he received a coin, he placed it on the bench in a small pile and looked at it. One time when he was looking at it, big tears filled his eyes, falling on the pennies, nickels, and dimes. They were men's tears, heavy.

Then the strangest thing happened. The coins on which his tears fell became fantastically beautiful. Again I found myself lost in God's silence, and felt as if the whole world had become mine. For a moment I seemed to exist and not exist at the same time.

I became aware of the beggar again. He turned his face towards me and I looked into his eyes. I had often read of the Transfiguration of Jesus on Mount Tabor, and something similar seemed to happen that day on that bench in that plaza. The beggar was transformed. He shone with a light that I could not endure, and his small pile of coins was transformed as well.

As in previous times, a voice came to me seemingly out of a wind. It said: "Catherine, this money, whether given out of abundance or out of scarcity, like the coins of the widow in the temple, is blessed. And those who gave it are blessed. But those who passed by and did not see you or me will not come to know my Father unless they repent. "Understand another mystery of the Trinity. I am teaching you as children are taught in first grade. My mysteries are not found in theology books. No, my mysteries are learned by loving me. Those who love me, and especially those who have come to the silver sands and have plunged into the sea of my infinity, they are the ones who learn the mysteries of the Trinity.

"It is time for you to learn more of them. You know a little about the mystery of God's mercy. Now you have to learn about the consolation of God. Yes, I became man, and like all other men, I sought, when I was on earth, consolation. I received very little of it, as have you. But see the little pennies and coins that people have given me. These are my consolation right now because they were given out of love for me. Love is the consolation of the Holy Trinity.

"Enter into this mystery, and understand that you console the Trinity through me. As you console me, you console my Father and the Holy Spirit, and my mother as well. So, do not forget: I was a man, and I sought consolation, and I did not receive very much. Nor will you if you are following my footsteps into my immense silence. My silence is the silence of people who desire to console their God."

Before I could say a word—I was awestruck by the transformation of this poor man—he was gone. But the little pile of money was still there. Out of the wind came his voice again: "Take this money and give it to those who need it. It is blessed." Then I was enveloped by the silence again.

I sat a long time on that bench, and many poor people came to sit beside me. To each one I gave part of this holy money, though they did not know it was holy. For a long time I entered into what I thought was the total silence of God. Of course it was not total. In our relationship with God there is always more. But at that time it seemed to me that I was touching the furthest depths of the silence of God.

Towards evening, a policeman came and said to me, "Woman, you have been sitting here all day. Move on, now." I said, "Can't I sit here all night too?" He replied, "Well, yes, if you want to. But you haven't eaten all day. I have some sandwiches my wife gave me. Here, take them." Then he left.

I became lost, not in the consolation of God, but the consolation of man. I seemed surrounded by a crowd of silent people, poor people. They were pressing in on me. My heart was open to everyone, for those who enter the great silence of God lose the key to their own hearts. Anyone can knock and walk in. The whole world was coming at me.

Then I noticed that they were wounded people, and realized that the whole world was wounded in one way or another. The rich were wounded by their riches, and the poor by their poverty. Everyone, without exception, was wounded.

It was a night without stars. People thronged silently around me and this time it was not Christ who was begging; it was all these wounded people. Each person extended both hands towards me, and in a whisper that turned into a rhythmic song, begged me to cure their wounds. They said their wounds were unendurable.

It was a most frightening thing! An innumerable crowd all begging, with extended hands, to be cured. I don't know anything about curing. I could pray for them, but curing, no. That was not my gift in the silence of God.

So I began praying for them. I prayed the prayer Jesus taught us: "Our Father, who art in heaven, hallowed be thy name. . ." The whispering changed. The hands were still outstretched, but slowly everyone began repeating the prayer. I quickly realized that not everyone had known the prayer. There were Muslims, Jews, people of all faiths, in the crowd.

I said, "Lord, what shall I do with all these wounded people? I cannot understand why *everyone* is wounded. No one seems to have escaped the deep spiritual wounds inflicted on them by the world. What is it? What must I do?"

It seemed that I was being pushed against a wall by all these people, and there was no place to go. They clamored in many languages and in a variety of ways. My heart was filled with prayer for them and I cried to God to come and help. I recited the psalm, "Out of the depths I have cried to you, O Lord. Help me! You promised you would!"

I thought of the Good Samaritan. But he had only one person to help and here were millions of people, each crying out to God for help and comfort. And while they were crying out, Satan was walking proudly around. He had a smile on his lips. He knew that these wounds were capable of leading people down the road to perdition.

I thought, too, of Job, and of how difficult it was to heal his spiritual and physical wounds.

Suddenly I heard a voice, the strongest voice I have ever heard. There was a field of poppies close by, and a man clothed in white sitting among the poppies. The wind picked up his voice and brought it to me as on previous occasions. I heard him say, "Blessed are the poor. . ." When he finished the beatitudes there was a deeper calm and joy among the people.

But they still seemed unsatisfied, as if they needed something else to salve their wounds, some balm that was not present in the words of the beatitudes. Majestically, the man in white stood up, and he was revealed as Jesus Christ. Many of the people still did not know who he was.

He told his apostles to lay out fish and bread. Then he fed the millions who surrounded me. After he had finished feeding them, hundreds of baskets of leftovers were taken away by those who had eaten. They were consoled by the food. But there still remained something that was not completely healed.

Then I saw another table being laid out. The apostles were loading these tables with huge quantities of bread and wine. "Oh," I said to myself, "now he is *really* going to feed them." And so he did. He fed all those millions with his own Body and Blood. There was no distinction between Jew and Muslim and Gentile. He fed those who knew who he was and those who didn't, fed them with this food of eternal life. He had died for all people, so he fed all peoples, and healed all.

At this the people vanished. I looked at him once more and he said to me, "Catherine, this is another mystery of God which you must learn. I love all mankind and I have reconciled all mankind to myself. This is why I came into the world, to be crucified and to reconcile all mankind to my Father. Go and spread this Good News to everyone."

The Mystery of the Church

The entire scene changed. I was in a large room that resembled a cathedral, like Hagia Sophia in Constantinople. A large number of priests were assembled, priests from every century, from the earliest days of Christianity until the present.

They were talking with each other; some were arguing. Some seemed about to come to blows! They were defending something. It reminded me of some of the councils of the Church in which, I had read, there were fierce arguments. I chuckled a bit at the absurdity of it, but then I started to cry. A sense of fear enveloped me.

I seemed to be perched on top of a colonnade so that I could look down and witness all this. What I saw brought both a joy and a terrible sorrow into my heart. The crowd of priests suddenly parted, and through the aisle thus formed came a procession of light–filled people in two long columns. I realized that all were saints. Tremendous light poured from them, and this light sought to penetrate the hearts of the priests. It entered those with open hearts, but others it could not penetrate.

At the very head, and in the center of the two columns, walked Mary, Queen of all Saints. The two columns represented the canonized and the uncanonized saints, and she is queen of both.

I recognized some of the faces: St. Augustine, St. Francis of Assisi, St. John of the Cross, St. John Vianney, and others. When I saw them reach the altar, a great joy overcame me. It was as if God said to me, "You see, I have saints, people who have followed me to the very end." St. Stephen came into view. I heard his beautiful words, "Lord, do not hold this sin against them."

In both columns were thousands of martyrs who had passed through the fire of blood. A great hymn arose. It did not break the silence of God, but it was heavenly music. Overwhelmed by his silence which enveloped this music, I fell prostrate before the Lord, whom I did not see but of whose presence I was aware.

As the music continued, my joy grew greater and greater and blended with the very joy of God. This is part of the mystery of the silence of God. It is really *sobornost*, man's union with God. Man begins to feel a little of what God feels—his joy and sorrow. It seemed that my heart would break, so heavenly was the music.

While the procession advanced I was recalling how we make distinctions between "beatified" saints and "canonized" saints. However man imagines these distinctions, they do not work that way with God. A saint is a saint! In one column were saints canonized by God long before official canonization by the Church. There were, for example, Mary Magdalen, and St. Peter, who was called "the Rock" by the Lord, and upon whom he built his Church, and Zacchaeus, and many others.

The music was joyous—the song of people who are forgiven, who are reconciled with Christ, who realize that they are sinners although they had been created in the image and likeness of God. They had followed Christ and his word in their own humble and hidden way.

In this procession were myriads of women who, down through the ages, had tended the sick, fed the poor, and taken from their own mouths bread to feed these poor. No doubt you would have recognized many of these people. Saints live among us all the time! What a beautiful sight it was, and the music was exquisite.

I saw St. Thomas Aquinas step out from the line of saints and ask his superior about burning his theological works. He said he had seen God as he was praying before his crucifix. From that moment he considered his writings as straw. I asked myself, "How did St. Thomas learn the mystery of God?" He had written so profoundly about the mysteries of the faith.

The answer came to me as if spoken by Christ: "The way to know me is not through books, but to pray and to do as did the woman with the issue of blood. (Luke 8:43–48) She pulled at my garment so that I would turn around and notice her. Catherine, this does not mean that you should put aside the intellectual gifts which I have given you and others. No. You must use all my gifts all the time. My Father has given them so that humanity might progress towards a peaceful life on earth.

"The way to learn about my mysteries is to be very silent, very quiet, and to wait. Then one day I shall come and reveal my mysteries to those who awaited my coming."

My surroundings changed again. I was alone and looked around. All the lakes and rivers were polluted. The fields smelled of chemicals sprayed by an airplane.

A fear entered my heart. I did not like the place. The silence captivated me but the surroundings did not.

I wanted to leave, yet I wanted to remain in the great silence of God. When one is in God's silence, places do not really matter, for one speaks with him, intimately. Entry into God's silence eventually results in a mysterious speech with him. This has to be experienced to be understood. It is a form of sobornost, in which one is united with God by the thin but strong thread of silence.

The wind came again, lifting me up and placing me in a large city. From there I made a pilgrimage, traveling, in a flash, thousands of miles and visiting hundreds of cities. I found myself immersed in everydayness, now among families, now talking to married couples, now surrounded by youth, now by the aged. At one point I walked along assembly lines in factories.

To traverse the world the way I was doing seemed to take centuries, and I became tired. I found the Holy Spirit asking me to rest and to pray about all I had seen, and especially about Christians. I was only too glad to comply.

How can I express my reaction? In response to everything that I had seen, I began to cry. In the silence of God my tears flowed, and they filled the earth. A small body of water appeared, which gradually grew into a river. And this river of my tears went straight through the world. What good it did I don't know, but I could not stop crying. That was my first reaction when the Holy Spirit told me to be still and pray about what I had seen.

One cannot analyze these things, only experience them, and that only in a small way. Do not imagine that there was any tremendous vision. There was simply an attempt to follow Christ. I knew that Christ had also cried. Perhaps this crying was a deeper entry into his silence.

I continued to think about what I had seen. Though there were tears on my face, the Tempter came. It seemed that I was in his hands, and he presented to me a very "logical" argument.

"Now, Catherine," he said, "It is time you yourself forgot all this 'silence of God' nonsense and started living, really living, in the time you have left. Live comfortably and peacefully. Use your time for yourself."

It was as if an evil wind was whipping all around me. Trees bent and broke in the force of it. I was shaken like a reed in that wind, and all the time the whisper of the Tempter was in my ear: "Why spend so many years in trying to bring the gospel of Christ to people who never listen? It all goes in one ear and out the other. Look at their actions. Those are proof of the uselessness of it all."

The storm and wind were frightful. What he was saying was partly true, and I asked myself, "How is it possible for the Tempter to be truthful?" I invoked the name of Mary and made the sign of the cross, and the wind subsided. Then like a weary traveler, I went to sleep. When I awoke, the Lord was there. He said, "You have been tempted because I need persons who are tempered like steel."

Again I found myself in different terrain. From a vantage point in gentle mountains I saw the Church. It is not "churches" that arise out of the silence of God but *the Church*. There she stood, above the tree line, shining in the rays of the noonday sun. She was beautiful and simple, with her doors wide open, and into her streamed rich and poor alike. As I beheld the Church, awe took

hold of me. These words from the Old Testament came
to me: "Take off your shoes; the place is holy."

A fire began to rage around her. Indeed, the place
was holy and so was this fire, for it was the fire of which
Christ had spoken: "I have come to cast fire upon the
earth, and I will that it be enkindled." I looked into the
fire and saw a Roman soldier pierce Christ's side with a
lance. From his body came forth blood and water. At that
moment I knew from whence the Church had been born.

The Church was a beautiful building; its walls were
transparent, as were doors and dome. Through its doors
walked all kinds of people, in great simplicity and in joy
of heart. Then I heard a great sound, the united voice of
the people of God. I knew beyond all doubt that this
people was joined to Christ; he was their head and they
were his members. A deep sense of adoration flowed
from this people into the silence of God. It was so overwhelming that I could hardly bear it.

When I looked again, the scene had changed. A
disruption, a dismemberment or tearing apart seemed to
be taking place. The doors through which so many
people had passed were being barred. I shook my head
and tried to clear my eyes, for they were filling up with
tears. I couldn't believe that the people of God were
causing all this turmoil! But they were. Each had his own
idea of the Church. "Intellectuals," who were supposed
to be supporting the Church, were arguing against her.
Some were even denying the existence of God.

As my father had taught me to do, I lifted the 'two
arms'—of prayer and fasting—for the Church.

At the same time I realized that the Church was the
beautiful, shining, Bride of Christ. He had said that the
gates of hell would not prevail against her. I knew that

she was his beloved, and that he, God, was all tenderness, all love, towards her. She passed in front of my eyes, the beloved of God.

Not only was she his beloved but she served the people whom he loved, the poor. The people whom he had fed with loaves and fishes she now fed with bread and wine. From my soul rose an immense cry of adoration.

Yes, I saw the Church torn apart. I was going to weep, but then I saw Christ putting her back together again, she who had come from his side. There was music in the air, and she became whole again.

So I was at peace for a little while, because I knew that the Church is forever being restored and renewed in her Lord. We celebrate his resurrection from death once a year, but he restores his Church every moment of the day and night.

I relaxed among the pines. It was night. Brighter than all the stars and the moon was the Church, shining in the darkness. I heard a voice say, "Once more, Catherine, you are tasting my immense silence. I want you to see the mystery of the Church. People may tear it apart, but I put it back together again. Have faith in my power. Your faith may seem to hang by a very thin string, but I will strengthen that slender string because you have to defend my Church."

The Multicolored
Vocation of Silence

A forest of Russian birches and tall fir trees rose majestically on one side of me, while on the other were the plain fields that I loved so much as a child. They were filled with flowers and with all kinds of little creatures, like chipmunks, that are not a bit afraid of you. It brought back memories of my youth.

Then darkness descended, and memories of youth vanished. I could no longer see the birches, nor the fields. Towering above me were the tall pines that make a rushing noise when wind comes to caress them.

I was then transported to different places in Russia, and taken to all kinds of monasteries. I asked the monks, "How do you survive *molchanie*?" They smiled and said, "The hardest thing to survive is not molchanie but the speech of other people!" I came to understand that for them speech was trying, but they engaged in it because they understood their vocation to be "multicolored." One of them clarified, "That means that our vocation to silence has many aspects."

"What aspects?" I insisted. "I am trying to understand molchanie, the great silence of God."

He said, "Remember when you came to me years ago to receive a blessing? You and your husband were the first to come on that special day, the day I came out of thirty years of solitude and began to preach the gospel."

Yes, I remembered that day, many years ago, when Boris and I had visited a holy hermit in northern Russia. Afterward the peasants there had told us, "When he speaks, it's as if Jesus Christ speaks." He broke his silence to be of service to those who came to him. That was one of the colors.

Next I went to see St. Sergius, my favorite Russian saint, and asked him, "St. Sergius, can you tell me about the multicolored vocation to silence?"

He smiled in his long beard and said, "Oh, yes, it is very simple. It means that one is totally at the disposition of God. It is the vocation of total abandonment to God. His call then takes on different colors.

"Sometimes you are called into the depths of Christ's pain. Then the vocation becomes dark, because pain has a dark color. It may be in Gethsemane, or before Pilate. Christ's pain is very deep, and only a few are called to enter into it. Among these few are lay persons as well as monks.

"Christ's deepest pain on the cross was his rejection by those he had helped, forgiven, and cured of their wounds and illnesses. But this pain has to be experienced before one can experience the joy of Easter.

"Joy has another color: white, golden white. You become bathed by it and it seems as if your heart will burst in anticipation of your own resurrection. But there are other colors in the multicolored vocation of *molchanie*. Why don't you go to other monks, St. Seraphim of Sarov, for example, and ask him?"

So I went to St. Seraphim of Sarov and asked him about the multicolored vocation of silence. He said, "You already know about the darkness of pain and the whiteness of joy. There is also the color of gray. It is the vocation of eating with the poor, with 'good-for-nothings,' and of annoying the big shots and the rich.

"The vocation of grayness involves living the gospel in the midst of closed hearts, in the midst of people who do not understand the essence of the gospel. Grayness is knocking at doors that never open. It is hurling stones against walls that never fall down. Grayness is the vocation of trying to enter men's stoney hearts. We must embrace this gray vocation in the silence of God. Closed hearts are a tragedy.

"When you are clothed with these colors, you become a spiritual father or mother. You have a vocation to remain in the silence of God, and yet to speak. The latch on the door of your heart is never closed. Somebody may come and ask you to be his or her spiritual father or mother. Because this is your vocation, you accept. At one and the same time you remain in the silence of God and you speak. Spiritual paternity or maternity is in itself a multicolored vocation."

In my imagination I travelled to another monastery and asked about the multicolored vocation. The abbot blessed me and said, "Come with me." He brought me to the chapel and left me alone, saying, "Now ask *him* what the multicolored vocation is." I asked God. He smiled and said, "Well, little by little I will tell you about it and reveal all its colors. It will take you awhile to understand the mystery."

This is a poem I wrote, expressing what I learned about the multicolored vocation of silence:

A Pilgrim of Silence and Pain

What is my answer? Listen!
There is no use...
I cannot hide,
I am a pilgrim of silence and of pain.

You walked barefoot
On the dusty roads of Palestine,
The Palestine that was so small.
I, your pilgrim, travel on ships
         and planes.
On roads and streets, across the
         sea, the air, the land,
To which Your Palestine would
         be a little nook,
A square,
A tiny part of my immense
         kaleidoscopic whole.
                  And yet Your footprints are
                           everywhere.

And I
I walk in them.
My steps are slow
For I am wounded too,
Even as You...
By You, my love... for You,
And them.
The wounds drip, drop by drop
On ship, on land, and in the air.

My blood—or is it Your blood in
me?—falls everywhere.

Gone are the days of speech...
Of just and flaming anger,
Of words like swords in Your
          defense.
Today I speak in silence
And through my wounds—or are
          they Yours?—
Alone among the noisy crowds,
I am a pilgrim of silence and of pain.
And everywhere I leave a gift,
A drop or two of blood,
Not knowing anymore if it is
          mine or yours.

          I am a pilgrim seeking You
          Yet giving You to all.
          For it is You, my Lord
          Who meets me in each one I see,
                    or touch or pass.
          How strange and how incredible.
          A mystery so profound
          And I so small and foolish!

I lose you in so many, Lord
For they will not welcome You
          into their homes
And I run again, with wounds
          that bleed,
With wounds that gape
A little more with every step,

But I run on and on
For I must find You, and at the
　　　same time, I must give You
To all I see and meet and touch.

　　　　Yes, I must find You,
　　　　And give you to all
　　　　Through *Silence*
　　　　and through
　　　　Pain.
　　　　ALLELUIA!

The silent monks of Russia were not the only people I visited. The forest of tall pines and birches opened up, and deserts began to flow past me like one vast river. Sand, trees, vegetation, everything blended into one. The snows of the north seemed to flow into the deserts of the south. Hindu holy men appeared. I saw lofty mountains, where Tibetan wise men lived. On the banks of the Amazon I saw native medicine men who also stand at the edge of the silver sands.

I was on pilgrimage and it seemed as if God wanted me to see all the silent ones on earth. He touched my shoulder and said, "Go and discover the many faces of my silence, which flows from my Heart, the Heart of the most Holy Trinity, and encompasses the whole universe. Most people do not know of this silence because they do not take the time to enter into it. Go!"

Mile after mile I trudged, talking to so many silent ones that I lost count. All these people were ordinary, unimportant, 'little' people. One or two from each community had received the call to enter God's infinite silence. I followed them, plunging into the silence and into the heart of each person.

So utterly immersed in the silence of God were these people that you could almost touch it. It was as if he had taken them beyond all boundaries and placed them in a land where all lands meet. They were still on earth, yet it seemed they had left the earth. When you approached these silent ones you knew that they were at the edge of the parousia. Everything about them breathed the peace that reigns there.

A shimmering, cascading light, which they seemed oblivious to, emanated from each one. In the presence of the silence of these persons, the nature of violence is exposed. You can almost see violence stalking about in the night, trying in some way to stamp out the silent ones.

In my travels across the world I did see violence conquer some of these silent persons. In a word, I saw martyrs. Some of them were bedecked in glory, though their bodies had been tortured. Everywhere, the silent ones of God allowed themselves to be violated by violence. Yes, all across the world many silent ones were becoming martyrs and, strangely enough, my heart rejoiced. I didn't feel pity. I rejoiced because martyrdom is a cradle of faith.

An infinite joy overcame me, and I began to sing in a loud voice. Suddenly, right next to me, I heard the voice of the Lord, saying, "Catherine, keep on singing. Martyrdom is the greatest gift I can give to man, and the greatest gift man can give to me."

Silence is like a desert which has ripples in its sands, ripples resembling waves. Seen from the back of a camel, these sandy waves appear to be eternally trying to catch up with the waves which have gone before. When you walk through desert sands, they are often knee–deep. The temperature can rise to 150 degrees in the daytime, and drop to 40 degrees at night. To really see the moon and the stars you have to go to a desert.

The desert is beautiful, but for some reason you cannot pay attention to it. Perhaps because of its starkness, what confronts you is desire for martyrdom. This desire grows in the hearts of all who have stood on the shore of the silver sands and plunged into the immense sea of God's infinity.

Now I ask you quite simply: Who wants to be a martyr? Who wants to accept martyrdom for the sake of his or her Beloved, for the sake of Jesus Christ? And yet, there *are* people who look for it, pray for it, hope for it, welcome it.

Consider the early Roman martyrs in the coliseum and elsewhere. Who can count them all? We know some who have been canonized, but all who died for Christ should be canonized. Many not only forgave their persecutors but, like St. Stephen, implored the Lord not to hold the sin of their murder against them.

It is not easy to explain this desire for martyrdom. You must enter a whole new dimension and cross the bridge of God's silence into his love. It is because you are completely in love with him that your desire for identification with the Martyred Beloved reaches such incredible proportions. You stagger through the sands like a person intoxicated with love, seeking your Lover and yearning to hold onto him in whatever way you can.

Back and forth he walks the desert of your soul crying out, "Don't you know how much I love you?" You answer, "You are God. You understand. You brought me to your silence, and your silence brought me to your love. And now I want to identify myself with you completely. I want to die for you."

Your footprints become deeply imbedded in the desert sand. You continue walking, seeking that door. It isn't to everyone that the door from silence into martyrdom is opened. Martyrdom is the full flowering of silence.

When the Indians tortured Jean Brebeuf, it appeared that he didn't feel anything, or, if he did, he did not show it. Somehow he was already in heaven. Heaven is the complete and total identification with him who was martyred for us all.

Blood shed for God is the cradle of new Christians. However, this door of martyrdom can be illusory, a mirage in the desert. One needs great wisdom here.

But what else can now save the world? Prayer? Yes. Fasting? Yes. But ultimately only martyrdom can save the world, as it was saved by *the* Martyr on the Cross. This is why, when I cannot sleep at night, I walk the desert. I begin to realize that the final stage of my journey lies through that door into martyrdom.

You can open a newspaper today and read about modern martyrs—in South America, in Russia. When the moment of martyrdom arrives, the souls of men, women, and even children are given by God a new burst of spiritual power. At the one final moment, life surges into a magnificent torrent, the torrent of love. It is the torrent of a goal achieved: martyrdom for the sake of the Beloved.

Many Christians, Jews, Hindus, and others who have entered into the silence of God have understood this, but how many have persevered in that silence until it finally clothes them with its full radiance?

The heart of man seeks for solutions to his problems until no solutions are left. Then he discovers that his "I" must disappear, in a sense—must become totally identified with Christ in his silent service to mankind. Yes, there are many silent steps to take before one comes to the door of total identification. But when you arrive there, your heart, like those of the martyrs, will receive a new burst of love. A heart which is finally united with the Beloved has this impulse.

Scripture says, "Do not arouse, do not stir up love before its own time." (Song 3:5) Everything is quiet now, for two silences merge into one. The door is open. Those who pass through the door come out on the other side clothed in a mantle of blood. Jesus Christ walks up to them and welcomes them with outstretched arms. Bloodied and battered, they fall into those arms.

New life emanates from them. Their mantle of blood is transformed into a mantle of gold. Christ ceremoniously presents them to his Father, who rises from his throne and embraces them. The Holy Spirit hovers over them with immense joy and gladness.

This is the age of martyrs. Those who are willing to accept martyrdom must still pray for the grace to become martyrs. I have a priest friend whom I have known since his seminary days. He could be called a martyr because he was interned in a Japanese prison camp where three of his confreres were actually martyred. God touched his heart and now he has the *desire* for martyrdom. I pray for him, that he may some day become a martyr, because if he does, he will beget thousands of Christians.

I spoke to God about this and asked, "Do you really want me to pray that people—myself and others—become martyrs? He answered, "Of course you should pray for that. How else is the Church to continue!"

The landscape seems arid and desert-like, and winds whip mercilessly at bushes, causing them to snap back and forth. I am alone in the great silence of God, so deep, so still. I see infinite depth in his great silence, which is his speech. One does not understand this right away.

A feeling of terrible loneliness takes hold of me and there is nothing I can do about it. God seems to have vanished, or rather, I can't find him anywhere except in the battle between bushes and wind.

Then a stillness ensues, and reluctantly I enter that stillness for I have decided to follow God wherever he leads. All I have to do is push the bushes aside a little and enter their depths. Just as I once stood by the silver sands and entered the sea of infinity, so now I have to enter these dense bushes.

It is a simple act, yet strange. For what shall I find in the heart of these bushes lost in this desert? Slowly, feeling as if my arms each weighed a thousand pounds, I push the bushes apart and discover a stairwell. Holding onto my cane, I descend into the heart of the bushes.

Each one of the seemingly bottomless steps reminds me of a step in the apostolate God has given me. On the first step I saw myself as a young woman walking briskly, happily, with a little attache case, a typewriter, and a bag with a few pieces of clothing. I was walking from my apartment on Isabella Street in Toronto, to Portland Street, where I would begin my apostolate.

Before my eyes arose the whole picture of my early apostolic years, with their poverty and begging. Another step, and I remembered my involvement in social justice. Then I looked down and couldn't see the next step. I had to jump! I came to our Friendship House on Rochester Street in Ottawa, where I used to get up at 5:30 A.M. and work until 11:00 P.M.

I couldn't see the next few steps either, so I jumped, seemingly into a void. As I jumped I had the impression of soaring and felt God's hands hold me very gently and place me safely on another step. It was Harlem, and my interracial apostolate there.

It's a long story—the story of my soul and of God's love. In Harlem it included contacts with Dorothy Day of the *Catholic Worker*, Father John Lafarge—a pioneer in interracial justice, and innumerable others.

Descending still further, I recalled the tall pines and birches of Combermere, and Bishop William Smith, who invited me to begin an apostolate here, in his diocese. I sit on the sand by the river running past our house, sit more still than do the insects waiting for their prey. While they wait, I listen to the wind in the bushes and talk to God.

Don't be astonished, my friends, at this revelry with God, for there are fools who talk with God once in a while! I am one of these fools. In Russia we call them *youródivui*, which means fools for Christ's sake. Yes, I am one of them. I speak to God in the darkness of the tall pines and white birches.

God said to me, "Catherine, do you remember your mother's words?" I asked, "Which, Lord?" He replied, "When she told you that you were born under the shadow of the cross." "Oh yes," I said, "I remember that very well." He continued, "That is where you are now. All the storms you have been subjected to were of the evil one. But I am here, and he cannot reach you, because you have passed from the silver sands into the infinity of my silence.

"At a very young age you fell in love with me. My Father and I and the Holy Spirit hovered over you. And my mother, whose child you are, was always with you, singing lullabies. You did not understand all that then. I saw the road that you would take, but I could not compel you to take it. It had to be journeyed freely by you.

"Slowly, as the years went by, because you loved me, you followed that path I had arranged for you. Oh, you zigzagged a little when you were young, but then the path straightened out. Now you continue to walk with questions in your mind, but only in your mind. Those questions I can easily answer. Tell me, Catherine, do you love me, my Father, the Holy Spirit, and my mother?"

When I nodded my head, overwhelmed by what he asked, he said, "That's all that matters. So never be astonished at being rejected or at being whipped or crowned with thorns, or at carrying your cross. Don't be astonished. You want to follow me. You are following me, and I am always nearby."

With these words he put my head on his shoulder, and began patting my hair. Well, I must admit that I was really "out of myself." His hands were calloused but soft, and I let myself go into the arms of God.

The Silence of Old Age

I feel closed in. I have reached the age where people hem me in on all sides. I am not free anymore. I cannot take an airplane and go to Europe if I want to. In many ways I cannot dispose of myself. Everything in me seems to be tied up. I walk with small steps. I used to be able to walk out into the woods and see many kinds of landscapes. I roamed up and down mountains and valleys. I was free. But now I feel all bound up. "When you are older you will stretch out your hands, and another will tie you fast and carry you off against your will." (John 21:18) Now I have only one landscape: the heart of God.

But how stupid of me to talk like this, I who have stood at the edge of the silver sands and jumped into the infinity of God's silence. I'm letting the old smother the new! I am losing myself in the past, and God looks at me going over my life.

Somehow it never occurs to us that tomorrow or the day after, our steps will falter, that we will be too weak to do what we would like. And yet, I think this 'unfreedom' of old age is also an entry into the silence of God.

God offers us many silences: the silence of babyhood, of childhood, of youth and maturity, and finally the silence of old age, with its accompanying lack of exterior freedom. My own heart must learn to accept this lack of freedom. People undoubtedly say about me, "She's old now. She can't do this and she can't do that." This is good, because now I enter a new depth of silence, and the very essence of poverty, for which I have so longed. Now I am exceedingly free.

In the past I tried to live, Lord, according to your will. As I bowed my head to your will I lived in the silence of obedience. Your speech, your will, was all light for me, no matter if it was pain or joy. All that came from you was beautiful, and I felt free. To be in your will, Lord, is to be in your silence and to have a freedom that no one can understand.

Until now, when I wanted to travel, I would make reservations and go. It is no longer so, but a new freedom has come into my soul. Yes, I am more bound in some ways, but I am also more free.

The earth is becoming a narrow sliver, of no more importance. Heaven is opening before me. This is the goal I always wanted to attain. No wonder earthly landscapes pass out of view.

God has given me a new key to the landscape of his heart, and nobody can stop me from entering it. Oh, people can herd me into this or that plane, put me into this or that room or hotel. But, ah, they cannot tame my wild and immense spirit, which needs no other landscape than the heart of God.

Here we are together, he and I. He, too, is bound. Bound with nails. They hurt much more than the soft bandages that are used to bind me. Perhaps he binds me so as to keep me close to him. When I feel myself bound, a window is always left open to me, and I can go and lose myself in God.

Yes, as I prayed today I saw that the Lord had removed all scenery, all earthly panoramas, and had given me a new one—himself. Previously, I had travelled over seas and mountains and deserts. Today I entered the immense scenery of God's own heart. My whole life, from babyhood until now, passed before me.

Russian babies were always bound in swaddling clothes by their nurses or mothers. I don't remember the joy of having free limbs as a baby! Mine were always bound. Then one day the Lord touched me, as with a wand, and I became free of the bonds. My baby clothes fell off and I found myself pumping my little legs—happy, gurgling, all excited. I was delighted.

My parents allowed me to be free, but within a strict discipline of love and understanding. I was never free as people are here, to do whatever they want, when they want, as they want. No, there were always boundaries.

When I was about two years old I was put in a harness when we went out to walk. I was somewhat free, but still in the power of my mother and father. All during my growing up, I became increasingly free from bindings, but never completely free.

I fell in love with God, and when you are in love with God there is full freedom to do what he wants.

Thus, surrounding me all my life was this strange lack of freedom on one hand, and total freedom on the other. At one and the same time I grew up in the midst of a total discipline and a total freedom.

Then came my marriage and the war. I passed from the simple life of a child to that of a young adult, and thence to the life of a mature person who submitted herself voluntarily to the discipline of God, as expressed by people in charge of me in one way or another. I was in love with God. And under the discipline of my parents and of the Church, I was tremendously free.

I would have to say that, in general, I was an exceedingly obedient person. The landscape I walked in this early part of my life was simple, ordinary, gray, with a few flowers strewn along the way. Obedience gives birth to flowers for those who walk her path. Oh, I wasn't perfectly obedient. Far from it! But nevertheless, I can say that I was an obedient person.

Now I have reached my eighties. People in their eighties usually are not obedient to anyone! But I feel that obedience is still at my side and I am under the supreme obedience of the Lord.

I feel I have finally attained poverty, of the kind I always dreamed about. My time now is God's time. I have an intense desire to pray, and to fast. Yet I know that neither fasting nor prayer is the most important thing, but rather to *be a prayer*, and to go about the world doing good to mankind as long as I possibly can, as long as my fingers can move and my mind is clear.

Thus, while I feel bound by my lack of freedom in my old age (something like the swaddling clothes I had on as a baby), I am beginning to realize that this is being done by God. He looked down on me and saw a lot of 'insects' that still needed to be killed—the insect of pride, the insect of desiring to be free in the wrong way. He put his hand on these insects and they died.

Who are these people binding me? Everybody in my apostolic family. Oh yes, they are doing it out of love, but still it is hard. It is thus that the Lord prepares the infant, in her old age, to enter the kingdom of heaven!

I am lost in the tenderness of God. It is a very wonderful thing that a human being can be filled with, and encompassed by, the tenderness of God. His tenderness is always there. But there are so many things that draw our attention away from God that his tenderness towards us often passes unnoticed.

When you have entered the great silence of God, everything changes. All that mattered yesterday does not seem to matter so much today. In fact, one looks for a moment at yesterday and wonders how it was possible that one's attention could focus so absorbingly on the utterly unimportant things that make up the warp and woof of our lives.

Now, clothed with patience, which is part of God's love for us, we sit very still. On the table before us lies the wool cloth, as it were, of our lives. Here, on this corner of the table, lies death. All our lives we were so afraid of it. But why? Probably because most people consider it to be the end.

Their fear of death is overwhelming. The fact that we shall lose our hold on existence as we know it, terrifies the majority of us. But for the few who have warmed their souls on the silver sands and have plunged into the infinity of God's immense sea of silence, that no longer terrifies.

The Lord wants us to love as he loved, so he made us his children and heirs. To those who want to see with the eyes of faith, he reveals the truth about death. Physical death is not the end. After death we shall enter into true life, eternity, where we can really be ourselves, instead of forever using masks to hide our real faces.

How sad are those masks you see in coffins! Perhaps for one fleeting moment before their death these persons cried out, "Why did I use this mask instead of being myself? Why did I not reveal that which should have been revealed? Why did I hide what should never have been hidden?" Then, on this last thought, their eyes closed in death.

There is a moment when God gives us a key to the mystery of life. We always had a key to his heart, and he always had a key to our heart. But this is a special key. It is the key of *wisdom*, which allows us to live a good life. We need this key to guide ourselves amid the noises of the world. We need it to choose what is wise.

One of the things that Satan does is confuse, and his favorite confusion is to substitute earthly wisdom for divine wisdom. Many are caught on this bait. But with the key of wisdom one can avoid such pitfalls. And this key can unlock many doors, even doors that men have invented when evil and madness have taken hold of them, doors that block their own true progress.

When you die, this key will die with you; no one who is looking through your effects will ever find it. Then it will no longer be necessary to you. But throughout your life it is a wonderful guide. Hold on to it! The key of wisdom is given to those who have plunged into the infinity of God's silence—or, to put it another way, it is given to children. Only children can possess this key.

"Grown–ups" cannot hold onto it; they let it slip through their fingers. Their intelligence stands in the way of the simplicity necessary to use the key of wisdom. Children know how to play with this key and, as they do, their knowledge grows. These "children" might have white hair and white beards. They now belong to the kingdom as "little children."

After you enter the silence of God, a most marvelous thing begins to happen, impossible to describe. There are no words to express the beauty, joy, and pain of this experience. It is as if one were already in the parousia!

For a second, there is a backward glance at the kenosis, or self-emptying, through which you have passed. You notice that it was a complete emptying of yourself. The false self seems never to have existed. The kenosis seems a small price for all that God has done for you.

The whole of your life now falls into two parts: the kenosis—the time of pain and problems; and the time of childhood, when you began to understand God's speech, when your mind and heart and soul became wide open to his Word. The key has done its work. You are wise, and this wisdom will grow in you, for you have the key to all its chambers.

There is a wonderful relaxation of soul and a patience that enters one's being. There is greater understanding. For having become possessed of the key of wisdom, you now "see" without seeing, and "hear" without hearing. It seems you have touched something like the hem of the Father's garment.

At this juncture you seem to pass out of yourself. It is not a question of dangling between heaven and earth. Rather, it's as if an immense hand gently enfolded you and lifted you higher and higher. You are able to hear a choir of angels singing to a Child, singing with joy, and you become part of this rejoicing.

Then, peacefully, someone puts you in your bed. The angelic choir ceases and a beautiful voice begins to sing a lullaby. All this happens when you accept the key of wisdom. He who plunges lovingly into the infinite sea of God's silence, and opens its treasures with the key of wisdom, has finally reached the goal. But the goal is a cross, and in the distance one sees men selecting nails.

The cross comes because the key of wisdom gives a power to look into men's hearts.

People come, one after the other, asking questions and demanding answers. They crowd around me in an ever-increasing throng, and cry out for me to be an intercessor between them and God. I do not quite understand it all—partly because they speak so rapidly. They look sickly and miserable.

All are bound up with strings of different colors. One is pink and reddish—human respect. Another is green–envy, a desire to be better than others. A third is white, a color one would imagine to be symbolic of childlike innocence. But no, it is the drab, grayish white of indifference. Persons tied with this are wrapped up in themselves, living for themselves and no one else. They are indifferent to God, to love, to anything that really matters. Then there are other colors as well, symbolizing the seven capital sins, which impede growth of soul.

I hold the key of wisdom in my hands, look at it, and ask God if he really wishes me to have it. For by giving it to me he inflicts deep sorrow on my soul. Christ answers very simply, "You wished to follow me, and you are. I see the souls of men and I am showing you the depth of degradation in man that brings forth tears from my Father's eyes."

When I hear these words of his I begin to cry. I kneel down and put my face into his lap. I cannot stop crying. His hand is over my head and he strokes my hair and says, "Those who want to follow me totally have to be total. Catherine, do you know what it means to be total? It means complete self–emptying. It means crucifixion, but it also means resurrection.

"Always, always, every hour of every day, you have a choice—to accept or reject. So far you have accepted to follow me totally. It is up to you to continue. My Father and I and the Holy Spirit give you complete freedom to reject or to accept us, remember that."

So I look again at the key, and at the people clamoring for answers. I realize, with a new understanding, that there is only one way that I can bring the peace of God to these people, and that is face to face, person to person. Mass meetings are of no avail. Lectures and speeches pass in one ear and out the other and are soon forgotten.

There may be a few exceptions, but basically there is only one way to bring people to God, and that is to love each individual personally. It is to love each one totally, completely, utterly.

Loving does not necessarily mean liking. Take the key of wisdom and unlock your own heart. Then let people in, one by one. Listen to them with full attention, with all your mind, heart, soul and body, unto exhaustion. The exhaustion will be lifted, and you will be able to listen still more. Yes, love must be communicated person to person, otherwise it will not be effective.

The End of All Waiting

It is impossible to convey what waiting on God or waiting for God means. Of course, God is always present; God is always with us. He is always coming to us, but we are not always awaiting his arrival.

There is a kind of waiting that is anxious. Take the parable of the workers in the vineyard. (Mt. 20:1–16) The owner comes several times and finds that there are still people who are waiting to be hired; I call them "the waiting people." But this is not the kind of waiting I am talking about. These people were anxious or annoyed or depressed. They had all kinds of emotions that are incompatible with the silence of God. Only in a broad sense can we say that they were waiting for God.

No, real waiting for him is quite different; it is quiet and peaceful. You are waiting for God to do something, although you don't know what it will be. There is immense joy in your heart. This kind of waiting is something like waiting for a loved one to arrive. Lovers pace back and forth when the beloved is even fifteen minutes late. They are nervous and excited, out of love and concern for the beloved.

Yet waiting for God isn't exactly like this. It is rather a tranquility, a certain tranquility that takes hold of you entirely, so that nothing stirs within you. You have only one thought: "He will come in his own time." There is a totality of peace.

All is quiet in one's heart. The mind is asleep but the heart is receptive. All emotions are subdued except the powerful emotion of love in one's heart. In this waiting for God, the totality of one's person is at peace. When this happens, God allows you to see why other people are not at peace and why there are so many problems. All the "whys" in the world seem to flash in front of you like a movie, but this does not disturb your own peace one iota. Rather, the "whys" incite you to pray for others and for their problems.

God has given us his own patience, to wait on him and to be ready for his coming. Do not be disturbed. The exact hour and minute of his coming lies in his hand and in the love of his heart. My task, your task, is only to wait without emotional storms, without impatience or pacing. In the totality of our person we are simply to be always expecting the footsteps of the Lord. Don't ever lose the immense peace of waiting for him.

Would that I could convey something of the peace, patience, and prayerfulness which comes from my own heart, the heart of one who has stood on the silver sands and plunged into the sea of God's infinity. I wish that I could convey it through my writings and talks, through any means of communication. But all means have proved useless for this; it is impossible to convey. All I can say is, "It is so."

At a certain time the Lord comes, bounding over the mountains like a person in love: "Hark! my lover— here he comes, springing across the mountains, leaping across the hills." (Song 2:8). Of course, this is poetic language; yet it is the true language of love.

Other poets have tried to put into words the experience of the Lord's coming—Francis Thompson, for example. In *The Hound of Heaven* Christ speaks here:

"All which I took from thee I did but take,
Not for thy harms,
But just that thou might'st seek it in My arms.
All which thy child's mistake
Fancies as lost, I have stored for thee at home:
Rise, clasp My hand, and come."

Yes, magnificent poetry, but even this falls short of expressing what happens at the Lord's coming. There are no adequate words to express the moment of the Beloved's arrival.

No longer is there any landscape; fire is all around me. I walk amid this fire as if compelled to, while seeking to understand why the landscapes have disappeared and why I am in the midst of these flames. The blaze raises me higher and higher, yet I do not see where I am going. I am beyond the earth now, beyond the planets.

A beautifully wrought chalice is placed into my hands. I look at it and its beauty overwhelms me. For a moment I either swoon or fall asleep. I am totally unaware of what is happening, except for one thing: that I am following God, am somehow entering into the heart of God. From seemingly far away, and yet ever so close, a voice says to me, "Higher, friend, come up higher."

I am also holding a staff, wonderfully carved, but without any precious stones. It is the staff of a poor shepherd. Staff in one hand, chalice in the other, I rise higher and higher. I look down at my naked feet and see that I am walking on a staircase of fire. The flames lick my feet without burning them.

Again, this is beyond my understanding and I ask, "Lord, what do you mean? How can I walk through fire and not be burned? I don't understand."

A voice answers, "Understanding! You don't need understanding. Turn around." I turn around and look back down the fiery staircase that I ascended and upon which I am still walking. I have left understanding far behind, on one of the stairs. Wisdom too is behind me, though not as far away as understanding.

Hope is my sole companion, here at my side. It looks like water, crystal pure. People approach me with all kinds of vessels to be filled with the hope that flows from me. I begin to feel the presence of someone so beautiful and powerful that I want to embrace him; but he seems always a few fiery steps in front of me.

I am holding the chalice from which water is flowing. I notice that the feet of the people who are coming to drink from the chalice are not burnt either. They do not seem to notice that there is this fire all around me that continues to lift me towards the summit of this mountain I am supposed to climb.

The chalice is overflowing, and from it people are drinking water and wine. This water and wine had seemed to come from me, but I see now that they do not. They come from God. I stand in the middle of this fiery staircase and cannot go any further. I see that the chalice not only has water and wine in it, but bread as well. And hungry and thirsty people continue to come and be fed.

A voice says to me, "Let them drink and eat." I do, yet the chalice remains full. Slowly, with a clarity of vision that I never possessed in my life, I begin to understand what is happening to me and the reason for my existence.

The fire which surrounds me brings me great joy. In the midst of this fire, I now see a tree. I watch this tree of faith grow, as people come and drink the water and wine and eat the bread. The flames recede a bit, enough that I can lie down and rest in the immense shade of the tree of faith.

I seem to forget everything, and yet remember everything. At my side I recognize both hope and love; they have grown to immense proportions. A voice speaks: "This is your life of hope and love. Now give me the chalice and set down the staff."

In the midst of that fiery landscape, filled with the most beautiful singing I have ever heard, I see two hands take the heavy chalice. Then a man comes near me and says, gently and tenderly, "Drink," and so I do. As I look at the hands which offered me the chalice, I say to him, "Your hands have been pierced." His voice becomes even more tender as he says, "Yes, for you and for all mankind. Drink what remains in the chalice, then come and rest your head upon my heart."

I do as I have been told. Then I know what very few people know—ecstasy.

Again the silver sands and infinite sea of God's love and silence appear. This time I come across a small village; it is Nazareth, and I am there like one seeking a lost treasure. I sit down beside a little pond where people are coming to wash their laundry. In this poor and humble place I seek the great silence of God.

But the place is fairly noisy and I cannot find God or his silence. I am very tired, so I find some shade and fall asleep. But the sleep is not restful. My heart is tortured and cries out, "God, where are you? I want you now, for I have made this long journey. I want to rest in your silence, my Lord."

I awaken and follow a dusty road, which has a strange beauty about it. From around a bend, a young woman comes walking towards me. I stop, and she stops, too. I say to her, "You are the one I am seeking. You can lead me to my love. I want to speak with him. I believe that the only way I can speak with him is by silence. The farther I walk into his silence, the more I have been able to hear his voice."

She looks at me with a lovely gentleness. There is a stone nearby. She points to it and says, "Come, sit down here with me. Yes, you have found me. I truly am the gate that leads to him whom you love. Hold my hand and I shall become a gate for you to pass through. I am the woman wrapped in the silence of God."

As she opens her arms, I see that the inside of her mantle is crimson red. She is the spouse of the Holy Spirit! Without hesitation I walk into her heart. And in this immense heart of the woman who is Mother of God and Mother of men, I meet him whom I love and seek.

Pax Caritas

I am a woman
    wrapped in
      Silence too.
For silence has become
    attire and song!
Silence is golden
    with light exploding
    as you become one with God
    and so do I.

        I am a woman
            wrapped in silence too.
        Silence has become
            for me
        Attire and song.

About the Author

Catherine de Hueck Doherty was born into a wealthy family in Russia in 1896. Many different strands of Christianity were woven into the spiritual fabric of her family background, but it was from the liturgy of the Russian Orthodox Church, the living faith of her father and mother, and the earthy piety of the Russian people themselves that Catherine received the powerful spiritual traditions and symbols of the Christian East.

At fifteen Catherine was married to Boris de Hueck. Soon they were swept into the devastating battles of World War I, where she served as a nurse. After the Revolution of 1917 they endured with all the peoples of the Russian Empire the agonies of starvation and civil war. Eventually Catherine and Boris escaped to England. At the beginning of her new life in the West, Catherine accepted the teachings of the Catholic Church, without rejecting the spiritual wealth of her Orthodox heritage.

In 1921 the couple sailed to Canada, where Catherine gave birth to their son George, soon after their arrival in Toronto. As refugees, they experienced dire poverty for a few years but soon Catherine's intelligence, energy, and gift for public speaking brought her to the attention of a large lecture bureau. Her talks were popular all across Canada and the United States. Within a few years, she became an executive with another, international lecture service. She became a North American success story.

In the 1930's, after several years of anguish, Catherine and Boris separated permanently; later the Church annulled their marriage. As devastated as Catherine was, she knew that God wanted something new from her now, but she did not know what it was. The words of Christ haunted her: "Sell all you possess, and give it to the poor, and come, follow Me."

Catherine took a room in a slum section of Toronto and began to quietly love and serve her neighbors, becoming their friend, and praying, hidden in their midst. But when others saw her and heard her speak, they wanted to join her. There was an intensity to her faith and love that lit a flame in the hearts of many men and women. Catherine had not envisaged a community, but when the Archbishop told her that, yes, Christ was calling her to this, she accepted, and soon Friendship House was born.

The works of Friendship House were modest—a shelter for the homeless, meals for the hungry, recreation and books for the young, a newspaper to make known the social teachings of the Church. Catherine initiated an interracial apostolate in Harlem, living with and serving the African-Americans. This work expanded to other cities: Chicago, Washington, D.C., and Portland, Oregon. Friendship House became well known in the American Church.

Catherine shared with her friend, Dorothy Day of the Catholic Worker, the intense struggle to move the Gospel out of books into believers' lives. Even if a few friends, such as the young Thomas Merton, recognized in her the power of the Holy Spirit and an unwavering fidelity to Christ's Church, many others were frightened by her Russian bluntness. Others simply could not grasp the largeness of her vision, especially because her experience of the ways of God were so foreign to them. Finally after a painful difference of opinion over the nature of the Friendship House Apostolate, Catherine found herself pushed again into the chartless waters of the Lord.

This time Catherine did not have to start alone. In 1943 she had married Eddie Doherty, a celebrated newspaperman, after he convinced her and her bishop that he wanted to share and support her vocation. In 1947, then, Catherine and Eddie came to Combermere, a small village northeast of Toronto, where the Bishop of Pembroke had agreed she could work among the rural families.

Again others came to join Catherine, and this time priests came to stay as well. The apostolate, now called Madonna House, grew slowly, but by the year 2000 Madonna House has more than 210 members, including twenty priests. The apostolate has foundations in Russia, England, France, Belgium, Brazil, Grenada, Ghana and Liberia, in addition to fourteen others in Canada and the United States. The training center in Combermere, Ontario offers an experience of Gospel life to hundreds every year.

As Catherine's inner life deepened and the community matured, she shared the fullness of the inner vocation Christ had formed in her. On the eve of the Second Vatican Council in 1962, Catherine established the West's first poustinia—a desert place of fasting and praying for unity, in, with and through Christ, a unity "that could only be the fruit of love." Her book *Poustinia* was awarded the prestigious *Prix Goncourt* of the *Academie Français*, and has been translated into dozens of languages; it witnesses to her spiritual depth and passionate zeal to pass on her faith in God.

Catherine died in 1985, a woman who had become a spiritual giant by responding to grace.

If you would like to learn more about Catherine Doherty and Madonna House, please visit our Internet web site at: www.madonnahouse.org

About the Cover Painting

The scene is set on the island on which Catherine lived for many years after the founding of Madonna House in Combermere, Ontario. The island gradually became for her, and for those who knew her, the symbol of her interior life and the place where the gift of Eastern spirituality was formulated for the West. Faced with today's complexities, Catherine dug deep into her roots to find the key for humanity to return to the Father.

Her cabin, or *poustinia*—shown in the foreground of the illustration—was named after the great St. Catherine of Siena. It had been previously designed and built by Nicholas Makletzoff, a Russian architect, craftsman and artist.

It was in this setting that Catherine interiorly returned to her roots. The poustinia became *a meeting place with God.* It was a simple building: a large cross dominated the interior; an icon of the Trinity hung on the wall; the bed was made of plain boards, with a minimum of padding. For nourishment, there was bread and water, or tea; and food for the soul— Scripture and silence.

In *Molchanie* we are invited to enter the silence of God, which is none other than his heart. By entering the sea of silence, one can yet preach the Gospel and draw an innumerable host of people to God. Many times during her life, Catherine Doherty was to cross the bridge between the world of God and the world of humankind, through embracing his infinite silence.

The painting was created in 1993 by Patrick Stewart, a member of the Madonna House Apostolate.

Also by Catherine Doherty

Madonna House Classics Series:

Poustinia: Encountering God in Silence, Solitude and Prayer
Sobornost: Experiencing Unity of Mind, Heart and Soul
Strannik: The Call to the Pilgrimage of the Heart
Molchanie: Experiencing The Silence of God
Uródivoi: The Prophetic Call of a Modern Fool for Christ
Bogoroditza: She Who Gave Birth to God

Other Titles:

Apostolic Farming
Beginning Again
Dear Father: A Message of Love to Priests
Dear Seminarian
Dearly Beloved: Letters to the Children of My Spirit
Donkey Bells: Advent and Christmas
Experience of God, An
Fragments of My Life
God in the Nitty-Gritty Life
Grace in Every Season
In the Footprints of Loneliness
In the Furnace of Doubts
Light in the Darkness
Living the Gospel Without Compromise
My Russian Yesterdays
Not Without Parables
On the Cross of Rejection
Season of Mercy: Lent and Easter
Soul of My Soul
Stations of the Cross
Welcome, Pilgrim

MADONNA HOUSE PUBLICATIONS

COMBERMERE • ONTARIO • CANADA • K0J 1L0

The aim of our publications is to share the Gospel of Jesus Christ with all people from all walks of life.

It is to awaken and deepen in our readers an experience of God's love in the most simple and ordinary facets of everyday life.

It is to make known to our readers how to live the tender, saving life of God in everything they do and for everyone they meet.

Our publications are dedicated to Our Lady of Combermere, the Mother of Jesus and of His Church, and we are under her protection and care.

Madonna House Publications is a non-profit apostolate of Madonna House within the Catholic Church. Donations allow us to send books to people who cannot afford them but most need them all around the world. Thank you for your participation in this apostolate.

To request a catalogue of our current publications, please call (613) 756-3728, or write to us at:

Madonna House Publications
2888 Dafoe Rd, RR 2
Combermere ON   K0J 1L0
Canada

You can also visit us on the Internet at the following address:

www.madonnahouse.org